WHY AMERICA MATTERS

A children's book about the Judeo-Christian values
of America and its founding, and the importance of the
Four Pillars of the American Cornerstone Institute:
Faith, Liberty, Community, Life.

by DR. BEN CARSON
with VALERIE PFUNDSTEIN

Illustrated by LIZ BALL

To my mom for instilling in me the values
that inspire me every day to be a better American.
—B. C.

To everyone who proudly flies the American flag,
reminding us all that patriotism begins at home.
—V. P.

Text copyright © 2021 by American Cornerstone Institute

Illustration copyright © by American Cornerstone Institute

Illustrated by Liz Ball

Published in the United States by
American Cornerstone Institute and Pfun-omenal Stories

Printed in the United States

All rights reserved.

First edition, 2021

ISBN 978-1-7378684-0-8 (hardcover)
ISBN 978-1-7378684-1-5 (paperback)

Books are available in quantity for premium or promotional use.

About the Authors

DR. BEN CARSON is a famous doctor who has saved many people's lives—including kids. He ran for President of the United States and served as a member of the President's Cabinet for four years, where he helped American families get housing. Dr. Carson and his wife, Candy Carson, are proud parents, grandparents, and Americans.

VALERIE PFUNDSTEIN has been a teacher, scout leader, mother, and a patriotic American who has written and published children's books, including Veterans: Heroes in Our Neighborhood, and now, with Dr. Ben Carson, Why America Matters. She and her husband, Paul (retired FDNY), are the proud parents of three children.

Flying high both day and night,
it's waving to us below.
America's flag matters.
Why do you think that is so?

The flag's our country's symbol.
We hold it dear to our heart,
reminding us of values
that have mattered from the start.

Matters of faith, liberty,
community, and life, too...
pillars make our country strong
and guide everything we do.

God lives in us through our faith,
shining brightly our own way
Unseen, yet we know He's there,
and faith matters every day.

Faith's a matter of the heart.
From the heart we always lead,
treating our neighbors nicely
as we care for those in need.

The pillar of liberty
matters because we are free
to share our thoughts and feelings
even if we disagree!

We're all free to be ourselves
and live life as we deserve.
Liberty matters greatly.
It's a freedom to preserve.

We take care of where we live,
the neighborly thing to do.
When communities matter,
our great country matters, too!

We keep our homes, schools, and streets
safe and clean as they can be.
So that neighbors can be proud
to live together happily.

The most precious pillar, life,
God's finest blessing of all.
Without life, nothing matters,
from the big to very small.

Our lives matter from the start
before any breath we take.
Care for one another's health.
Protect life, for goodness sake!

Two sides of coins, heads and tails,
different, but the same worth,
Just as the founder's voices
mattered at our country's birth.

Look at the proud bald eagle.
Wings matter, both left and right.
If same or if different,
both are needed for its flight.

Your ideas are special.
We don't all have to agree.
I'm glad to know your feelings.
That matters so much to me!

I'll matter the same to you.
Thank you for letting me share!
When you take time to listen,
it shows me how much you care.

This country is not perfect
and each day we grow some more.
Does America really matter?
In our hearts, we know for sure.

Yes, America matters,
and the four pillars do, too.
Live them each and every day
to celebrate me and you!

Getty Images

George Washington

© Billy Graham Evangelistic Association. Used by permission. All rights reserved.

Reverend Billy Graham

FAITHFUL AMERICANS

Getty Images

Abraham Lincoln

Getty Images / Keith Lance

Harriet Tubman

AMERICANS
OF LIBERTY

Getty Images / Keith Lance

Betsy Ross

© The Louis Zamperini Foundation

Louis Zamperini

COMMUNITY LEADERS

Getty Images / National Archives

Clara Barton

American Cornerstone Institute

Dr. Ben Carson

PROTECTORS
OF LIFE

Place personal
photo here

Place personal
photo here

Faith

Liberty

Name _____

Name _____

Place personal
photo here

Place personal
photo here

Community

Life

Name _____

Name _____

THE "PILLARS" OF MY NEIGHBORHOOD

About the American Cornerstone Institute

Why America Matters is part of the Little Patriots Program
produced by the American Cornerstone Institute.
Guided by the cornerstones of
FAITH, LIBERTY, COMMUNITY, and LIFE,
the American Cornerstone Institute (ACI)
works to strengthen the bonds that hold
our country together through educational programs
and by promoting conservative, commonsense
solutions to the issues facing our society.

LITTLE
PATRIOTS